JOURNEY OF DECISION

A Way of the Cross

Sarah A. O'Malley, O.S.B.
Robert D. Eimer, O.M.I.

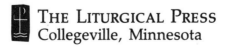

THE LITURGICAL PRESS
Collegeville, Minnesota

Journey of Decision
is dedicated to our parents,
Ida and Michael O'Malley and
Fred and Anna Eimer

Illustrations by Sr. Mary Charles McGough, O.S.B.

Scripture quotations are taken from the *New American Bible with Revised New Testament,* copyright © 1986 by the Confraternity of Christian Doctrine, Washington, D.C., and are used by permission of copyright owner. All rights reserved.

ISBN 0-8146-2016-7

INTRODUCTION

In the Gospels many people are involved in the death of Jesus, some more directly than others, like the priests, the Pharisees, the Romans, the screaming mob. Some individuals are known by name—Judas, Herod, Caiaphas, Pilate. Unfortunately, the Gospel writers did not reveal the thoughts of the people involved in the passion drama. Nonetheless, we know that the people involved in the crucifixion were confronted with the difficult decision: to accept or reject Jesus.

Fr. Henri Nouwen, a noted spiritual writer, remarks that, in encountering the Cross, people throughout the ages have always been confronted by the choice either of becoming Christ's followers or his executioners. This is true today. When we face the Cross in our lives, we make choices that determine whether we become followers of Christ or his executioners.

Similarly, through our sins, we all share some responsibility for the death of Jesus. Jesus is the Lamb of God who takes away the sins of the world—not just the sins of his day but of all ages. In that sense, we were all there on that day of darkness.

Journey of Decision is a Way of the Cross intended for both individual and group use. Either way, the following comments might prove helpful.

1. The spirit of *Journey of Decision* is involvement. The dramatic form (the fourteen monologues) engages our imagination. The Scripture texts at the beginning of each station, with a few exceptions, set the scene for the monologues. Each station focuses on a character who was intimately involved with Christ's passion, and who indirectly questions us about our own involvement. The characters not only invite us to look at their strengths and weaknesses, but also challenge us to examine our own strengths and weaknesses.

The use of imagination is important. Most of the characters used in the monologues are found in the traditional Way of the Cross—for instance, Pilate, Simon, Veronica. However, a few characters are not common to the traditional stations and must be imagined. For example, Barabbas, in station two, can be imagined as scowling around the edges of the crowd as he delivers his monologue.

2. *Journey of Decision* uses the following method:
   A. The traditional refrain of "We Adore You, O Christ" announces the station.
   B. The character is named and an appropriate quotation from the Scriptures sets the scene.
   C. Each station highlights a particular character, who, in monologue fashion, responds to the penetrating question, "Were You There?"
   D. In the concluding prayer of each station, the individual or group responds reflectively to what was revealed in the monologues.
   E. Verses of the song "Were You There?" are interspersed throughout the Way of the Cross; however, other songs could be substituted.

There are three ways *Journey of Decision* can be used for groups.

The first is the traditional way. The priest or leader reads the monologues and the congregation responds as indicated. For variety, other men and women could dramatically read some of the monologues.

Journey of Decision can also be used for small groups (in retreat or classroom setting) by having the entire group move from station to station. Volunteers could place themselves under the stations and become the various characters rendering the monologues. The monologues might be read well or memorized.

Finally, *Journey of Decision* would be very effective for a large congregation. Adults or students in the sanctuary could act out the fourteen stations. For instance, Jesus and Pilate would be in the first station. The actors would be frozen until the time of the monologue when Pilate would come alive and render his monologue. By the time the congregation responds with prayer, Barabbas would replace Pilate for station two and freeze until the time for his monologue.

Jesus' character could be played with minimal actions, or with almost symbolic postures. For the third station, Jesus drops to his *right*

4

knee, at the seventh, to his *left* knee, and at the ninth to *both* knees. Jesus would extend his hands for the nailing and close his eyes and drop his head for the twelfth station. Although it would be better that the monologues be memorized, it is not necessary as long as they are read with skill and feeling.

The following cast is suggested for the stations:

Station	1	Jesus and Pilate
Station	2	Jesus and Barabbas
Station	3	Jesus and Herod
Station	4	Jesus and Mary, Mother of Jesus
Station	5	Jesus and Simon of Cyrene
Station	6	Jesus and Veronica
Station	7	Jesus and Caiaphas
Station	8	Jesus and a woman
Station	9	Jesus and Centurion
Station	10	Jesus and unrepentant criminal
Station	11	Jesus and Dismas (the good thief)
Station	12	Jesus and Magdalene and Mary, Mother of Jesus
Station	13	Jesus and Salome and Mary, Mother of Jesus
Station	14	Jesus and Nicodemus, and Joseph of Arimathea

Any props or special lighting have to be used tastefully. Simplicity helps: for instance, a chair is sufficient for Pilate, or a dagger for Barabbas. Much is left to a director's or leader's imagination. If needed, the number of actors could be cut down by having them play several roles.

We thank Rose Lee Eilering, Barb Kaiser, and Wanda Martin for their typing of the manuscript and Mary Bilby, Sr. Lucille Geisinger, O.S.B., and Jo Ann Yeoman for their constructive criticism. Finally, we thank Sr. Mary Charles McGough, O.S.B., for her illustrations.

Sarah A. O'Malley, O.S.B.
Robert D. Eimer, O.M.I.

OPENING PRAYER

LEADER: Lord, after being condemned to death by Pilate, you began your long journey to Calvary. The people you encountered along the way either accepted or rejected you. Pilate and Herod turned their backs on you, whereas, Mary, Veronica, and the Centurion accepted you.

As we begin this devotional Way of the Cross, we also are making a journey of decision—to accept you as Lord and Savior or to reject you. By listening to the thoughts of the biblical characters who met you along the way, may our hearts be moved to hear your call—a call to change, and to follow you. Amen.

LEADER: FIRST STATION—PILATE CONDEMNS JESUS
We adore you, O Christ, and we praise you

PEOPLE: **Because by your Holy Cross,**
you have redeemed the world.

PILATE

LEADER: "When Pilate saw he was not succeeding at all, . . .
he took water and washed his hands. . . ."

PEOPLE: **"I am innocent of this man's blood.**
Look to it yourselves." (Matt 27:24)

Of course, I was there at the trial. History will probably say I could have prevented the Nazarene's death, but put yourself in my position. Those Jews were a horrible nation of people—hardheaded, violent and contemptuous. There was never any pleasing them. Once, when I brought portraits of the emperor into the Jewish temple, the Jews complained to the emperor himself. Even Rome feared their fanaticism and did not back me when I took action against them. I had only one thought—advancement out of this uncivilized, backward nation. Then the Jewish leaders brought a harmless rabbi to be put to death. This Jesus told me he was the Son of God. I am a superstitious man—I don't deny it—I don't like prosecuting gods, even Jewish ones. So I did my best to free him. Instead the mob begged for a murderer, a certain Barabbas, to be set free. Well, imagine what it was like to hear that mob shout: "If this man goes free, Pilate, you are no friend of Caesar." Yes, another report to the emperor would have meant the end of my career. After all, a person must think of himself. You get ahead by playing the court game—wouldn't you agree? So I condemned him. If you had been there, would you have done differently?

LEADER: Let us pray . . . .

PEOPLE: **Jesus,**
        blind ambition is no stranger in our lives.
        Without your help,
        we, like Pilate,
        are capable of betraying the innocent.
        Remind us that in betraying the innocent,
        we are betraying you.
        May we never make others our scapegoats,
        no matter how powerless or disabled they may be.
        Give us strength to say "No" to the group
        when we are pressured into being thoughtless and
            cruel to others.
        May the clamor of the mob never overpower the quiet
            voice of our conscience.
        Amen.

Were you there when Pilate washed his hands?
Were you there when Pilate washed his hands?
Oh! Sometimes it causes me to tremble, tremble, tremble!
Were you there when Pilate washed his hands?

2

LEADER: SECOND STATION—JESUS ACCEPTS THE CROSS
We adore you, O Christ, and we praise you

PEOPLE: **Because by your Holy Cross,
you have redeemed the world.**

BARABBAS

LEADER: "Therefore I shall have him flogged and then release him."

PEOPLE: **"But all together they shouted out,
'Away with this man.
Release Barabbas to us.'"** (Luke 23:16, 18)

Call me Barabbas or whatever name you wish. I watched the Nazarene as he took up his cross and I saw him fall again and again. You might ask, "Why did I follow him along the way?" It wasn't that I became his disciple. It was just that I was curious. Anyone would be curious about a person who became your free ticket out of jail. Frankly, I didn't understand the man. He didn't act like a Messiah at all. I can appreciate hatred—vicious, cutting hatred. In fact, I had killed Romans and I fully intended to do it again until every Roman was driven from our land. But Jesus! He didn't hate the Romans or intend to kill them; he didn't curse the soldiers as they put a crown of thorns on his head. Instead, after his trial, he stood there like a lamb as they spit on his face. Then he accepted the cross without a murmur, like a person predestined to carry it. I guess I don't understand anyone who doesn't fight back or hate his enemy. Yes, I was there on that Friday. Were you there also?

LEADER: Let us pray . . . .

PEOPLE: **Heavenly Father,**
your son was destined to die in place of Barabbas.
Beyond that,
it was your plan that Jesus die for all of us.
He became the Lamb of God,
sacrificed for all people.
Lord God,
we are free to choose new life
and to receive this wondrous gift of salvation.
At this present moment,
we gratefully accept the death of Jesus
which has freed us from the prison of sin
and offered us new life.
Amen.

Were you there when he bore the wooden cross?
Were you there when he bore the wooden cross?
Oh! Sometimes it causes me to tremble, tremble, tremble!
Were you there when he bore the wooden cross?

3

LEADER: THIRD STATION—JESUS FALLS THE FIRST TIME
We adore you, O Christ, and we praise you

PEOPLE: **Because by your Holy Cross,
you have redeemed the world.**

HEROD

LEADER: ". . . Herod and his soldiers treated him (Jesus)
contemptuously and mocked him, . . ."

PEOPLE: **". . . and after clothing him in resplendent garb,
he sent him back to Pilate."** (Luke 23:11)

You ask me if I was there? Me, Herod? Of course, I was there. Out of my palace window, I saw him carry his cross and stumble to the ground. He once said, I'm told, that everyone needs to take up his cross to be his disciple. He had some message about serving others. What a fool Jesus was, babbling about sacrifice and selflessness! What did it get him but death? After all, what is life all about except for its many pleasures? Wouldn't you agree? To me, life is such a bore. Amusement is the only thing that relieves the boredom. But back to Jesus. I could have saved him, this rabbi, if he had only humored me. Had he just pulled a few tricks, showed me a miracle, or some magic. Who knows? Ha! I might even have followed him. But he turned out to be a simpleton, a silent one at that, who wouldn't even talk to me. Yes, I was there, and through my window I saw him crash to the ground with his cross. It seemed like the whole world was there. Surely you were there, too.

LEADER: Let us pray . . . .

PEOPLE: **Jesus,**
as Herod saw you struggling under the weight of
the cross,
he called you a fool.
You chose the cross
and refused to become his court jester and entertainer.
In our society, Lord,
it is easy to be pleasure-oriented and live for
the moment.
In challenging us to become your disciples,
give us wisdom to see the value of carrying our
daily Cross.
Amen.

Were you there when he stumbled to the ground?
Were you there when he stumbled to the ground?
Oh! Sometimes it causes me to tremble, tremble, tremble!
Were you there when he stumbled to the ground?

4

LEADER: FOURTH STATION—JESUS MEETS HIS MOTHER
We adore you, O Christ, and we praise you

PEOPLE: **Because by your Holy Cross,
you have redeemed the world.**

MARY, MOTHER OF JESUS

LEADER: " '. . . Your mother and your brothers are standing outside
and they wish to see you . . .' "

PEOPLE: **" '. . . My mother and my brothers are those
who hear the word of God and act on it.' "** (Luke 8:20, 21)

Here am I, his own mother, and I couldn't recognize him. The shock went through my body like the tremor of an earthquake as I saw my son, carrying a cross. Then Jesus found my eyes. Although I saw piercing pain in his eyes, I also saw peace. Suddenly all the earlier memories began to flood my soul—the memory of that day long, long ago when I said "yes" to a messenger of God. How could I have known then what that "yes" would cost me: fleeing with Joseph to save our child from a mad king's sword; searching all over Jerusalem for three days for our little boy. Nor could I ever forget the day when, as a grown man, he lay down his carpenter's tools once and for all. Of course, I was puzzled as he prepared to leave, saying those strange words, "I have my Father's work to do." Father's work! Was dying on the cross the Father's work? When I saw his bruised and swollen face, *faith* was all that I had left. Faith alone helped me accept God's will that Friday when the universe howled with insane laughter and darkness enveloped the sun. Jesus' eyes said to me on that Good Friday: "Believe in God; trust in a loving Father."

LEADER: Let us pray . . . .

PEOPLE: **Lord of the Universe,**
how difficult it is to accept a world
that includes people who are violent, selfish
and deceitful.
Sometimes it seems impossible to make sense out of
the confusion of life.
Then, like *Mary,*
we must cling to our faith and trust in you,
a loving Father who cares about each one of us.
We affirm your mysterious plan for our world:
that ultimately good will triumph over evil.
Lord,
in embracing the personal Crosses of our lives,
allow us to become not *bitter* persons,
but *better* persons.
Amen.

Were you there when he met his mother's gaze?
Were you there when he met his mother's gaze?
Oh! Sometimes it causes me to tremble, tremble, tremble!
Were you there when he met his mother's gaze?

5

LEADER: FIFTH STATION—SIMON HELPS JESUS CARRY THE CROSS
We adore you, O Christ, and we praise you

PEOPLE: **Because by your Holy Cross,
you have redeemed the world.**

SIMON OF CYRENE

LEADER: "As they were going out,
they met a Cyrenian named Simon; . . ."

PEOPLE: **". . . this man they pressed into service
to carry his cross."** (Matt 27:32)

I was coming in from the fields to do some trading when my curiosity led me into the crowds to see what the commotion was all about. Before I knew what happened, a Roman centurion seized me by the arm and forced me to carry a criminal's cross. Under my breath, I cursed my rotten luck—wrong place at the wrong time. I felt sorry for the poor fellow who was going to die on the cross, but I was mighty glad it wasn't me. Still I hated the weight of those wooden beams and the roughness of the road. So I asked myself, "Why has this happened to me, Simon, a poor farmer? Why do bad things always happen to me?" But then I saw the face of Jesus, a face I could never forget. He nodded his head as if to thank me. Suddenly the cross seemed lighter; it was no longer a burden for me to carry. Yes, this event was forever etched in my heart. As it turned out, I was in the right place at the right time, and I am thankful that I could help him carry his burden. What about you? Were you in the crowd that day?

LEADER: Let us pray . . . .

PEOPLE: **Jesus,**
Simon at first reluctantly shouldered your cross,
angrily resenting the burden.
Only with time
did he *willingly* assist you in the journey of the cross.
What he saw as misfortune
he later counted as a blessing.
Simon's reluctance and anger are a part of all of us.
Give us open hearts to see your presence
in the sick, hungry and homeless people of our world,
and give us generous hearts to respond to their needs
through works of mercy.
Amen.

Were you there when Simon shared his cross?
Were you there when Simon shared his cross?
Oh! Sometimes it causes me to tremble, tremble, tremble!
Were you there when Simon shared his cross?

LEADER: SIXTH STATION—VERONICA WIPES THE FACE OF JESUS
We adore you, O Christ, and we praise you

PEOPLE: **Because by your Holy Cross,**
you have redeemed the world.

VERONICA

LEADER: "When did we see you a stranger and welcome you,
or naked and clothe you?"

PEOPLE: **"Amen, I say to you,**
whatever you did for one of these least brothers of mine,
you did for me." (Matt 25:38, 40)

I had known Jesus only from a distance. I listened to his preaching and to his dreams of a kingdom where the wolf would lie down with the lamb. I heard his burning words of hope on the mountainside. I saw him heal others and I knew his special kindness toward women. I remember him saying once that when you give a cup of water to the least of your brothers or sisters, you give it to him. When I heard he was condemned to die, I hastened to be near the side of the road leading to Golgotha. I heard him groaning under the weight of a heavy cross. On his face were blood and grimy sweat. I pulled off my veil and ran to wipe his face. As a soldier raised his whip, I winced, but instead of lashing out, he shook his head in disgust and lowered his arm. The Master's bloodshot, piercing eyes encountered mine and seemed to say, "Thank you, Veronica!" As I removed my veil from Jesus' face, I was surprised. His gift for my small deed of kindness was a rough imprint of his face. I was able to help Jesus in my own way. What about you? Were you there when Jesus passed your way?

LEADER: Let us pray . . . .

PEOPLE: **Jesus,**
what a beautiful spontaneous gesture—
Veronica wiping your bruised and bleeding face.
Fearlessly, she seized the moment that would never
come her way again.
Make us spontaneous Christians who are not afraid
to take a risk.
Like Veronica,
may we comfort you when we discover you sick,
whether in the hospital or in the home.
May we find you in the faces of the poor and
suffering.
Remind us that the smallest kindness,
done for the least of our brothers and sisters
is done for you.
Amen.

Were you there when she offered him her veil?
Were you there when she offered him her veil?
Oh! Sometimes it causes me to tremble, tremble, tremble!
Were you there when she offered him her veil?

LEADER: SEVENTH STATION—JESUS FALLS THE SECOND TIME
We adore you, O Christ, and we praise you

PEOPLE: **Because by your Holy Cross,
you have redeemed the world.**

CAIAPHAS

LEADER: "Likewise the chief priests, with the scribes, mocked him among themselves . . . ."

PEOPLE: **"He saved others;
he cannot save himself."** (Mark 15:31)

I stood there along the road and saw Jesus fall a second time. He shivered with pain and exhaustion as he collapsed to the ground. It seemed like the drama would soon be over. I was only performing my duties as high priest when they brought Jesus to me and said, "Caiaphas, this is a dangerous man." Not only had he blasphemed by claiming to be God, but he had also misled and corrupted the people. Besides breaking the Sabbath, Jesus had predicted the destruction of the temple and had driven out money-changers on his own authority. After all, who was this Jesus but an ordinary laborer, an unlettered carpenter's son who had the arrogance to challenge our lawyers and rabbis? But, most important of all, I had to protect the nation. This so-called Messiah, who had a gift for deceiving the people, could destroy the peace and bring the Roman hordes crashing down upon us. Better that one man die than that the nation be destroyed. I saw Jesus fall that day and I wasn't sure he would ever get up again. Did you also see him fall?

LEADER: Let us pray . . . .

PEOPLE: **Jesus,**
in your journey to Golgotha,
you felt the weight of the cross and the mockery of the high priest
as you fell for the second time.
How quick we are to be self-righteous with people who challenge us.
How easily we condemn people
who didn't have the education or opportunities we had.
There are times that we, too,
feel burdened with the weight of the cross.
In loneliness, weariness, sickness, depression and misunderstanding,
we are sometimes brought low.
Make our yoke sweet and our burden light through your abiding grace.
Amen.

Were you there when he fell a second time?
Were you there when he fell a second time?
Oh! Sometimes it causes me to tremble, tremble, tremble!
Were you there when he fell a second time?

8

LEADER: EIGHTH STATION—JESUS MEETS THE WEEPING WOMEN
We adore you, O Christ, and we praise you

PEOPLE: **Because by your Holy Cross,
you have redeemed the world.**

WOMAN IN THE CROWD

LEADER: "A large crowd of people followed Jesus, . . ."

PEOPLE: **". . . including many women who mourned and
lamented him."** (Luke 23:27)

You won't get any name from me. It's safer to remain an anonymous mourner. I was part of a group of women who accompanied and cared for criminals condemned to be crucified. But Jesus was no ordinary criminal. Our leaders had accused him not only of breaking the law but also of being a blasphemer. And yet I was puzzled. How could a gentle harmless healer who had a reputation for doing so much good be condemned to such a cruel death? Who am I to judge?—me, just an ordinary mother. It was only when we met him on the way that we saw how cruel they were to him and I was touched. My tears became genuine. Imagine our surprise when he turned to us and said, "Don't weep for me; rather, weep for yourselves and your children." That alarmed me because his manner was that of a prophet. He seemed like a man with a message—a message that I didn't fully comprehend. I didn't understand the mystery about Jesus; yet I believed he was someone special, possibly the Messiah. What about you? What do you believe?

LEADER: Let us pray . . . .

PEOPLE: **Jesus,**
you met a group of weeping women along the way
**   of the cross.**
You told them to weep,
not for you,
but for the nation that would soon be cruelly
**   scattered by the Romans.**
Give us the eyes to see
and the ears to hear the prophets among us.
Lord,
grant us a compassion for others' sufferings
and a sincere sorrow for our personal sins
that have crucified you down through the ages.
Amen.

Were you there when the women wept for him?
Were you there when the women wept for him?
Oh! Sometimes it causes me to tremble, tremble, tremble!
Were you there when the women wept for him?

9

LEADER: NINTH STATION—JESUS FALLS THE THIRD TIME
We adore you, O Christ, and we praise you

PEOPLE: **Because by your Holy Cross,
you have redeemed the world.**

ROMAN CENTURION

LEADER: "When the centurion who stood facing him saw how he breathed his last, . . ."

PEOPLE: **". . . he said,
'Truly this man was the Son of God!'"** (Mark 15:39)

I was there, a Roman centurion, part of the most disciplined war machine in the world. I watched the King of the Jews as he crashed to the ground and was helpless to get up. Even now my guilt haunts me when I remember what we had done to Jesus in the courtyard: how we mocked him, crowning him with thorns, and played vicious games by striking his blindfolded face. It was my official role to make sure he would die on that Friday. He was just another criminal, another person to be crucified with Roman efficiency. But then I began to study this man—no, he was more than a man. It was far more than the darkness or lightning that influenced me—it was his manner. I had seen hundreds of men face death on the cross—they cursed and screamed. Jesus was different: he had a strange peace about him that went beyond my understanding. He forgave the people who taunted him under the cross. In the end, he died like a god, with dignity. Finally, under the cross, I was driven to my knees, driven to recognize him for what they said he was—the Son of God. I asked him to forgive me for my cruelty and hardness. I was there when he fell a third time. Were you there? Did you recognize him, too?

LEADER: Let us pray . . . .

PEOPLE: **Father,**
as Jesus fell a third time,
the Roman centurion discovered something deeper in
your son than mere humanity.
Rather,
he found divinity in the patience, goodness and
forgiveness of the Savior.
Almighty God,
we often look for an all-powerful god
to rescue us from our trials and our enemies.
Help us to find your presence
in the patience, goodness and forgiveness of others.
Amen.

Were you there when he struck the ground again?
Were you there when he struck the ground again?
Oh! Sometimes it causes me to tremble, tremble, tremble!
Were you there when he struck the ground again?

10

LEADER: TENTH STATION—JESUS IS STRIPPED OF HIS CLOTHING
We adore you, O Christ, and we praise you

PEOPLE: **Because by your Holy Cross,**
you have redeemed the world.

UNREPENTANT CRIMINAL

LEADER: "Now one of the criminals hanging there reviled Jesus,
saying, . . ."

PEOPLE: **". . . 'Are you not the Messiah?**
Save yourself and us.'" (Luke 23:39)

Watching Jesus get stripped of his clothing, I knew that I was next. I hated him because he didn't curse the Romans like I did. I despised him for his peaceful face. Finally, I mocked him because they said he was the Messiah. For if he were really the Messiah, he would have led our people to freedom from the scourge of these Romans. So, yes, I baited him. I tried to get him angry at the Romans—at me—at anyone. When I couldn't get him angry, I even begged him, "Save us, if you are the Son of God. Save us if you've got God's power." As a desperate criminal condemned to the cross, I would have done anything to save my hide. I wanted to live a little longer, but he seemed to welcome death as if it were a door to a greater life. I was there when he stood with dignity as the Romans humiliated him. He filled my soul with bitterness. Were you there watching also?

LEADER: Let us pray . . . .

PEOPLE: **Loving Father,**
in the eyes of a bitter criminal,
they stripped your Son, Jesus,
of his freedom and rights on the day of his trial.
Then they stripped him of his clothing before
they nailed him to a cross.
However,
they could not strip him of his dignity as your
Beloved Son.
Clothe us
with the warmth of a father's love
and an inner dignity as your sons and daughters.
Through the experience of your grace,
remind us that we are your family
even though we may wander far from you.
Amen.

Were you there when the soldiers stripped his clothes?
Were you there when the soldiers stripped his clothes?
Oh! Sometimes it causes me to tremble, tremble, tremble!
Were you there when the soldiers stripped his clothes?

11

LEADER: ELEVENTH STATION—JESUS IS NAILED TO THE CROSS
We adore you, O Christ, and we praise you

PEOPLE: **Because by your Holy Cross,
you have redeemed the world.**

GOOD THIEF

LEADER: "The other, however, rebuking him, said,
'. . . This man has done nothing criminal.'"

PEOPLE: **"Then, he said,
'Jesus,
remember me when you come into your kingdom.'"**
(Luke 23:40-42)

When they began nailing Jesus to the cross, I heard the gasps of pain and yet I heard no curse from his mouth. I told my fellow prisoner to keep quiet. We deserved what we got, but Jesus—well, he was different. From the days of my youth, I was a liar and a thief. Later I became a professional who stole for a living, and a murderer who had killed many Romans after joining the insurgents. The thought of right and wrong rarely passed through my head. But something in Jesus made me look at myself and face myself, maybe for the first time. People told me he talked about forgiveness and mingled with the rough crowd, the sinners, and that he promised a better life in another world. I didn't understand his mysterious kingdom and how it would come about, but I believed in it. Likewise he talked to god as if he were talking to his father. Yes, I saw Jesus open his arms and get nailed to a cross as though he wanted to embrace the world. I heard Jesus call my name, Dismas. Then he said, "This day you will be with me in paradise." I was there and became a believer. Did you become a believer, too?

LEADER: Let us pray . . . .

PEOPLE: **Jesus,**
as they nailed you to the cross,
you were like a lamb going to the sacrifice.
Instead of cursing your enemies,
you forgave them and excused their ignorance.
You offered salvation to a thief who repented.
Lord,
make us aware that your cross means forgiveness and
** salvation.**
Lead us to repentance of our sins
so that, like the thief,
we, too might join you in paradise.
Amen.

Were you there when he opened wide his arms?
Were you there when he opened wide his arms?
Oh! Sometimes it causes me to tremble, tremble, tremble!
Were you there when he opened wide his arms?

12

LEADER: TWELFTH STATION—JESUS DIES ON THE CROSS
We adore you, O Christ, and we praise you

PEOPLE: **Because by your Holy Cross,
you have redeemed the world.**

MAGDALENE

LEADER: "There were also women looking on from a distance."

PEOPLE: **"Among them were Mary Magdalene,
Mary the mother of the younger James,
and of Joses, and Salome."** (Mark 15:40)

I watched the life draining from Jesus—watched as he gasped for breath. Jesus had driven seven devils from me and had healed and welcomed me as a follower—me, Magdalene, a sinner, a woman. Yes, it was my sins, my weaknesses, that helped place him on the cross. I felt that. During the hours of his suffering, I understood what sin was—not just the sin of the Roman soldiers but my sins and every person's sins. Sin meant death; sin meant killing Jesus, my master; sin meant crucifying him to a cross. In some mysterious way, I understood what Jesus had done. He had taken my sins, our sins, and nailed them to the cross. As I gazed at his battered body, words of forgiveness echoed in my mind: "Father, forgive them for they know not what they do." And Jesus' words of forgiveness resounded in Mary's heart too, calling her to forgive those who had killed her Son. I was present and saw the agony of Jesus. Were you there when Jesus died for our sins?

LEADER: Let us pray . . . .

PEOPLE: **Jesus,**
what a sad moment when Magdalene stood under
the cross,
helpless to assist you, her Savior.
How grateful indeed was your mother,
to have Magdalene present in her time of pain
and sorrow.
Grant us,
not so much to be consoled as to console.
Call us to a change of heart
so that, like Magdalene, we might follow you.
Enlighten our minds to see that sin is harmful to us
and others.
But teach us that,
no matter how sinful we are,
we can be forgiven through your death.
Amen.

Were you there when he bowed his head and died?
Were you there when he bowed his head and died?
Oh! Sometimes it causes me to tremble, tremble, tremble!
Were you there when he bowed his head and died?

LEADER: THIRTEENTH STATION—JESUS IS LAID IN THE ARMS OF HIS MOTHER

We adore you, O Christ, and we praise you

PEOPLE: **Because by your Holy Cross,
you have redeemed the world.**

SALOME

LEADER: "Then the mother of the sons of Zebedee approached him with her sons . . . ."

PEOPLE: **" 'Command that these two sons of mine sit,
one at your right and the other at your left . . . .' "**
(Matt 20:20, 21)

My sons had fled. What irony that I, Salome, remained to watch the soldiers lay Jesus' dead body in his mother's arms. I touched Mary's shoulder while she cradled him as though he were a child again and rocked him to sleep. I felt ashamed when I thought of how I had asked Jesus to place my boys, James and John, at his right and left, in positions of power. Jesus had asked my sons if they could drink of the cup of suffering. At the time they didn't understand him, even when, during the Last Supper, he passed the cup of wine which would signify his coming death. My sons and the other apostles ran to safety in Galilee as Jesus carried his cross, alone. Only later would I realize why Jesus had to suffer and why my petty ambitions for my sons would seem childish and silly. Only under the cross did I understand why Jesus acted like a slave during the Last Supper and washed the feet of my sons. I was there when Jesus died and I thought of his cup of suffering. Were you there, too? Could you drink of his cup?

LEADER: Let us pray . . . .

PEOPLE: **Jesus,**
the last thing that Salome wanted for her sons
** was failure.**
In the eyes of an ambitious world,
to see you carry a cross and die like a criminal,
signalled complete failure.
In various ways,
we all cringe at the very thought of losing face,
schooled as we are in the American dream of success.
Lord,
prevent us from walking over people in order to
** get ahead.**
If we must compete,
let it be healthy competition.
Better yet,
let us work together to build a just Kingdom of peace
** and love.**
Amen.

Were you there when they took him from the cross?
Were you there when they took him from the cross?
Oh! Sometimes it causes me to tremble, tremble, tremble!
Were you there when they took him from the cross?

14

LEADER: FOURTEENTH STATION—JESUS IS LAID IN THE TOMB
We adore you, O Christ, and we praise you

PEOPLE: **Because by your Holy Cross,
you have redeemed the world.**

NICODEMUS

LEADER: "After this, Joseph of Arimathea, . . . asked Pilate if he could remove the body of Jesus."

PEOPLE: **"Nicodemus . . . also came
bringing a mixture of myrrh and aloes. . . ."**
(John 19:38, 39)

34

After preparing Jesus' body for burial, I helped Joseph, my friend, place Jesus' broken body in the tomb. In truth, Joseph was braver than I, asking for his body and knowing very well that the Sanhedrin and Pharisees, with wagging tongues, would take note of that action. I admired the Rabbi, but from a distance. When I met him, it was always at night under the cover of darkness, so that no one would see me with him. Call it human respect or whatever you want: I was afraid of what my peers might say or do if they knew I was attracted to Jesus. I secretly admired his teaching, too, even though he sometimes puzzled me—like when he said, "Nicodemus, to enter God's kingdom you must be born through water and the Spirit." But after the crucifixion, I no longer cared about risking my fellow Pharisees' displeasure. I was angry and ashamed that they had given Jesus over to the Romans to be crucified. I was even angrier at myself for not stepping forward sooner. I was there with Joseph when he placed the stone against the entrance of the tomb. What about you? Were you there on that dark Friday?

LEADER: Let us pray . . . .

PEOPLE: **Jesus,**
in the beginning of your public life
Nicodemus showed himself as a weak and timid
   follower.
Later,
at your own death he became an open witness.
Strengthened by our faith in your resurrection
and your conquest over sin and death,
make us bold followers and fearless witnesses to
   the Father's plan for us—
to bring about his Kingdom in this world.
Amen.

Were you there when they laid him in the tomb?
Were you there when they laid him in the tomb?
Oh! Sometimes it causes me to tremble, tremble, tremble!
Were you there when they laid him in the tomb?

CLOSING PRAYER

LEADER: Let us pray . . . .

PEOPLE: **Father,**
during our lifetime,
each of us makes a personal journey on the way
** of the cross.**
Similar to the characters we have seen,
we are confronted by many decisions *for* and *against*
** Christ.**
Renew within us the grace of baptism
so that we may choose to follow your son.
Enliven within us the grace of confirmation
so that, as your people,
made new by the Spirit,
we may become modern-day witnesses of your death
** and resurrection.**
Amen.

Were you there when he rose and conquered death?
Were you there when he rose and conquered death?
Oh! Sometimes it causes me to tremble, tremble, tremble!
Were you there when he rose and conquered death?